ABIDING IN HIM
Devotions for a Deeper Connection

Allan Lynfester

ABIDING IN HIM. Copyright © 2025. Allan Lynfester. All Rights Reserved.

Printed in the United States of America.

No portion of this book may be reproduced, stored in a retrieval system, or transmitted in any form or by any means, except for brief quotations in printed reviews, without the prior written permission of DayeLight Publishers or Allan Lynfester.

ISBN: 978-1-966723-22-6 (paperback)

Scripture quotations marked "KJV" are taken from the Holy Bible, King James Version (Public Domain).

Scripture quotations marked (NIV) are taken from the Holy Bible, New International Version®, NIV®. Copyright © 1973, 1978, 1984 by Biblica, Inc.™ Used by permission of Zondervan. All rights reserved worldwide.

Scripture quotations marked "ESV" are from the ESV Bible® (The Holy Bible, English Standard Version®), copyright © 2001 by Crossway Bibles, a publishing ministry of Good News Publishers. Used by permission. All rights reserved.

Acknowledgements

I would like to extend my gratitude to Ms. Crystal Daye and the team at DayeLight Publishers for creating the beautiful and captivating cover design, as well as for publishing this book. Their talent and expertise brought my vision to life.

I'm grateful to my family, friends, and loved ones, who supported me through the writing process. Your encouragement and patience mean the world to me.

Most of all, I thank God for inspiring and guiding me throughout this journey. May this book bring glory to Him and blessing to its readers.

Table of Contents

Acknowledgements iii
Introduction 7
Day 1: God is Our Help.. 9
Day 2: God Has Great Plans For You 11
Day 3: God Will Fight For You 13
Day 4: Put God First... 15
Day 5: It Pays to Obey 17
Day 6: Abide in the Word 19
Day 7: Always Give Thanks 21
Day 8: Speak Life... 23
Day 9: God Knows Best... 25
Day 10: God Wants to Do a New Thing 27
Day 11: Let God's Word be a Light for Your Path............. 29
Day 12: Spend Time in the Secret Place 31
Day 13: Give Your Cares to God.. 33
Day 14: Rest in the Lord 35
Day 15: Though We Fall, Yet We Rise Again..................... 37
Day 16: God's Love is Unconditional 39
Day 17: There is Power in Worship..................................... 41

Day 18: The Power of Belief...43
Day 19: We Have Power and Authority in Jesus...............45
Day 20: All Things Are Working For Our Good...............47
Day 21: Do Not Be Distracted 49
Day 22: All Things Are Possible...51
Day 23: We Need Each Other 53
Day 24: God is Our Healer..55
Day 25: Keep Your Focus on God......................................57
Day 26: God is Limitless...59
Day 27: Lead by Example 61
Day 28: Forgiveness is Essential...63
Day 29: God Will Put Your Enemies to Shame.................65
Day 30: God Will Blow Your Mind...................................67
Final Thoughts..69
Author Bio..71

Introduction

Welcome to Abiding in Him, a 30-Day Devotional journey designed to deepen your relationship with God and transform your life from the inside out. In a world filled with distractions, noise, and uncertainty, it's easy to lose sight of what truly matters, our connection with our heavenly Father.

As you embark on this journey, you'll explore the benefits of abiding in God, including unshakeable peace that surpasses understanding, joy that overflows from a heart surrendered to Him, spiritual growth that equips you for every good work, guidance and wisdom for navigating life's challenges, and strength and courage to stand firm in your faith.

Through daily reflections and scripture-based insights, you'll discover the power of surrendering to God's will and living a life that pleases Him. You'll learn to cultivate a consistent prayer life and listen for His guidance, trust in God's sovereignty and goodness in uncertain times, embrace the freedom and forgiveness found in Christ, develop a heart of gratitude, humility, and obedience, and experience the joy of living a life that honors God.

Each day's reading is a personal invitation to spend quality time with God, deepening your understanding of His character and love. You'll apply biblical truths to your everyday life, leading to lasting change and spiritual growth. You'll experience the transformative power of God's Word and presence, guiding you on a path of spiritual growth, hope, and purpose.

Take a step closer to God today, and let Him transform your life from the inside out. May these daily devotions guide you as you abide in the One who loves you most.

Day 1

God is Our Help

I will lift up mine eyes unto the hills, from whence cometh my help. My help cometh from the Lord, which made heaven and earth. (Psalm 121:1-2 – KJV).

No matter what you go through in life, the Lord is always there. Even when you don't feel like He's there, He is. If you call on Him, He will hear you and answer your call. He will never turn His back on you. He loves you unconditionally and will never neglect you. He will always help you in times of need. He promised to never leave you nor forsake you.

You may have struggles. You may have problems that you feel like you can't solve. You may feel like you're climbing a mountain that is insurmountable. In times like these, you should call on God. He will always come to your aid. He may not always make the problem go away, but He will give you the strength to endure it. You will emerge stronger on the other side. You will be victorious. Don't give up on God because He won't give up on you. He's able.

Always remember that God is the source of your strength. He is always ready to come to your aid. Call on Him. He will help you.

PRAYER

Heavenly Father, please help us to remember that You are always there for us. When we feel overwhelmed by the cares of life, we can always call on You. Please give us comfort and peace in the midst of our storms. Help us to stay rooted and grounded in You. May we always put our trust in You and rely on You for strength. In Jesus' name. Amen.

Day 2

God Has Great Plans For You

"For I know the plans I have for you," declares the Lord. "Plans to prosper you and not to harm you, plans to give you hope and a future." (Jeremiah 29:11 – NIV)

You may be facing challenges or struggles. You may feel like you're down on your luck. You may be in a dark situation in which you don't see a way out. Just stand on the promises of God. The Lord wants to prosper you. He wants to give you hope and a future. You may encounter situations that cause you to question the above scripture, but God doesn't lie. He only wants the best for us. He wants us to prosper in every area of life. It is up to us to put our trust in Him.

Our God is faithful. Put Him in first place in your life. Live a life of obedience to Him and watch your life transform. If you are faithful to God, He will be faithful to you. Live a life that pleases God. Have complete faith in Him. Develop a relationship with Him, and He will pour out His blessings upon you. It is not the will of God for His children to constantly struggle. God wants to bless you. All He requires is obedience. Live a life that is pleasing to Him. He will bless you more than you can imagine.

PRAYER

Heavenly Father, may we always remember that You have great plans for us. May we always live a life of obedience and submission to You. Please bless us and prosper us in every area of our lives. In Jesus' name. Amen.

Day 3

God Will Fight For You

The Lord will fight for you. You need only to be still. (Exodus 14:14 – NIV)

Y ou may have been wronged. You may have been criticized and slandered. People may have spread lies about you. There may be people who go out of their way to make your life miserable. You may be tempted to retaliate, but don't. Do not take matters into your own hands. You may be only adding fuel to the fire. Leave it to God. Let Him fight for you.

Even when you feel like getting even with others and giving them a taste of their own medicine, don't do it. Leave all vengeance to the Lord (see Romans 12:19). God will put your enemies to shame.

Whenever the Israelites put their trust in God, He gave them victory over their enemies. Put your trust in God. Surrender everything to Him. Let it go and allow Him to take control. Not only will He fight for you, He will also give you peace. Even when your enemies try to destroy you, know that God will fight on your behalf. Leave everything to Him. Pray to Him and leave everything at His feet. He is a just God who will not let evil deeds go unpunished.

PRAYER

Heavenly Father, please help us to remember that You will fight for us. We don't have to exhaust ourselves trying to get back at those who have wronged us. We surrender everything to You and allow You to take control. You have never lost a battle, and You never will. Lord, please fight our battles for us. In Jesus' name. Amen.

Day 4

Put God First

But seek ye first the kingdom of God, and his righteousness; and all these things shall be added unto you. (Matthew 6:33 – KJV).

It is human nature to try to do everything in our own strength. We sometimes burn ourselves out trying to achieve our dreams and desires, and even after we accomplish them, we still don't feel happy or fulfilled. We sometimes become frustrated when things don't work out the way we want them to.

We are sometimes filled with worry and anxiety when we think about our future. But the above scripture reminds us that we should seek first the kingdom of God, and all other things will be added to us. If you are a child of God, you have an advantage. God will give you uncommon, supernatural favor. You may get jobs you are not qualified for, unexpected opportunities, or blessings that you couldn't have imagined. God knows what you need. He knows your dreams and desires. Seek Him. Put Him first.

God rewards His children for their faithfulness. All He requires is for us to surrender our lives to Him and live a life of obedience. It will not always be easy. There will be trials and temptations. But if you are faithful to God, He will open the windows of heaven and shower you with blessings. Seek the Lord. You have nothing to lose.

PRAYER

Heavenly Father, please help us to put You first. At times, we are tempted to chase after the things of the world. Please help us to seek after You and the things of You. Following You is not easy, but it is worth it. Please help us to make You our number one priority and schedule our days around You. In Jesus' name. Amen.

Day 5

It Pays to Obey

And it shall come to pass, if thou shalt hearken diligently unto the voice of the Lord thy God, to observe and to do all His commandments that I command thee this day, that the Lord thy God will set thee on high above all nations of the earth. And all these blessings shall come on thee, and overtake thee, if thou shalt hearken unto the voice of the Lord thy God. (Deuteronomy 28:1-2 – KJV).

When we are obedient to God, He blesses us. Deuteronomy 28 tells us the blessings we will receive if we live a life of obedience to God. All He requires is our obedience. Surrender your life to God and live in a way that pleases Him, and He will shower you with blessings.

Deuteronomy 28 goes on to tell us the curses that will fall on us if we are disobedient. Sin may give us pleasure, but it comes with consequences. Every sin has a consequence. We may not feel the effect immediately. It can be weeks, months, or even years afterwards, but until we repent and turn from our sins, the consequences will catch up to us. It pays to live holy. God loves us and wants to bless us. Live a life that is pleasing to Him and watch the blessings unfold.

PRAYER

Heavenly Father, please help us to be obedient to You. Please give us the strength to live righteously and avoid sin. Sin may be pleasurable, but it is not worth losing our souls. Please help us to seek after righteousness and holiness. In Jesus' name. Amen.

Day 6

Abide in the Word

For the word of God is quick, and powerful, and sharper than any twoedged sword, piercing even to the dividing asunder of soul and spirit, and of the joints and marrow, and is a discerner of the thoughts and intents of the heart. (Hebrews 4:12 – KJV).

The Word of God is a powerful weapon. It is the sword of the Spirit. The devil and his legion of demons hate when we read the Word of God. They will use every strategy to keep us from reading the Word. We need to saturate ourselves in the Word of God.

When we are rooted and grounded in the Word, no evil will be able to triumph over us. Start speaking the Word of God over your situation. If you are sick, speak healing scriptures over your life. If you struggle with fear, speak scriptures about boldness. If you struggle with temptation, speak scriptures relating to your situation. When you begin to speak the Word, strongholds are broken, demons begin to scatter, and angels begin to work on your behalf. Always have your weapon ready.

Read the Word of God, meditate on it, and speak it over your situation. There is power in the Word of God.

PRAYER

Heavenly Father, please help us to abide in Your Word because it is food for our spirits and also our weapon. May we always saturate ourselves in Your Word. In Jesus' name. Amen.

Day 7

Always Give Thanks

Enter into his gates with thanksgiving, and into his courts with praise: be thankful unto him, and bless his name. For the Lord is good; his mercy is everlasting; and his truth endureth to all generations. (Psalm 100:4-5 – KJV).

As children of God, we should always have a grateful heart. We have so much to be grateful for. Instead of complaining, we should have an attitude of gratitude. Just the mere fact that we woke up this morning is enough reason to be grateful. When we constantly complain, we will inevitably find more things to complain about. However, when we have an attitude of gratitude, God blesses us by giving us more things to be grateful for.

Things will not always go the way we want them to, but we should remain grateful in bad times. No matter the situation, there is always something to be grateful for. 1 Thessalonians 5:18 reminds us to give thanks in all situations. When we practice gratitude, not only do we receive more blessings, but we also experience the peace and joy that the Lord brings. An attitude of gratitude helps us to be happy in all circumstances. Stop complaining and start being grateful.

PRAYER

Heavenly Father, You have been so good to us and we are so grateful. May we never be ungrateful to You. Please continue to shower Your blessings on me. Thank You for everything. In Jesus' name. Amen.

Day 8

Speak Life

Death and life are in the power of the tongue: and they that love it shall eat the fruit thereof. (Proverbs 18:21 – KJV).

There is power in the tongue. People take this lightly, but there is a lot of truth to it. We must be mindful of the words we speak. People often speak negatively about their lives without realizing the effect it has on them. The more negatively you speak, the more negative your circumstances will become. If you consistently say that you're stressed, broke, or nothing good ever happens to you, you will continue to experience that. However, if you consistently speak positive things over your life, you will experience positive outcomes.

No matter how negative your situation may be, keep speaking positively. Just as Ezekiel prophesied to the dry bones and they came back to life, we need to speak life over our dead situations. Eventually, things will begin to change for the better. People often speak curses over themselves without realizing it. Never speak negatively about yourself, even as a joke. Make positive declarations. The songwriter says, *"Speak over yourself, encourage yourself in the Lord."* The tongue is mightier than the sword. Use it wisely.

PRAYER

Heavenly Father, Your Word says that we shall decree a thing and it shall come to pass. Please help us to always speak positive things over ourselves. In Jesus' name. Amen.

Day 9

God Knows Best

A man's heart deviseth his way: but the Lord directeth his steps. (Proverbs 16:9 – KJV).

Our plans for our lives are not always God's plans for us. We may want our lives to be a certain way, but God leads us in a different direction. God knows what is best for us. He wants to prosper us and bless us.

Sometimes we are set in our ways. We want things our way and in our time. However, God knows the right path for us to navigate. He is all-seeing and all-knowing. We may be upset when things don't work out the way we want them to. The relationship that failed may be God's way of protecting you from an unhappy marriage. You may be upset that we didn't get a particular job, but God knew that you would have been miserable in that job.

We need to follow the Lord's leading. He sees the bigger picture. What we perceive as a disappointment or a setback may actually be God protecting us from harm. Trust the Lord. He loves us and wants the best for us. If He closes one door, He will open another. God knows best. If He leads you on a different path than you expected, it is because He has something better in store for you. Put your trust in Him. He won't let you down.

PRAYER

Heavenly Father, please help us to trust Your plan for our lives. When things don't work out the way we want them to, help us to remember that You know what is best for us. Please help us continue to follow Your lead and trust You wholeheartedly. In Jesus' name. Amen.

Day 10

God Wants to Do a New Thing

Behold, I will do a new thing; now it shall spring forth; shall ye not know it? I will even make a way in the wilderness, and rivers in the desert. (Isaiah 43:19 – KJV).

God wants to do a new thing in your life. We often feel stuck, but God wants to work in and through us. Sometimes God wants to do more in our lives, but we hold on tightly to what we have. It takes faith and trust in God to allow Him to work in us.

The above scripture states that God will make a way in the wilderness and rivers in the desert. There is nothing too hard for God to do. If He was able to part the Red Sea for the Israelites, dry up the Jordan River so they could cross, let the sun stand still for Joshua, and close the mouths of the lions for Daniel, He can do great and mighty things for you. Those are just a few of the many miraculous things God did in the past. Imagine what great and mighty things He can do for you.

Open your heart, trust Him, and fully surrender everything to Him. You will be amazed at the things that will work out in your favor. God wants to do a new thing for you. Just trust Him and let Him work.

PRAYER

Heavenly Father, we know that there is nothing too hard for You to do. Please help us to trust You wholeheartedly and allow You to do a new thing in us. Sometimes we lack faith, but please help our unbelief. Please help us to let go of our expectations and allow You to work in and through us. In Jesus' name. Amen.

Day 11

Let God's Word be a Light for Your Path

Thy Word is a lamp unto my feet, and a light unto my path. (Psalm 119:105 – KJV).

We need God's Word to direct our paths. In a world of darkness, we need the light of God's Word to lead us to safety. If you are walking at night in a pitch-black area, you won't be able to see where you are going. You need light so you can see the road ahead. Similarly, if you are not reading the Word of God, you are walking in darkness. You won't be able to see the way ahead, so you will stumble and fall. However, if you saturate yourself in the Word, you will be able to see the road ahead.

God's Word helps us to see in the spiritual darkness that surrounds us. God speaks to us through His Word. The Bible is a manual that teaches us how we should live. No matter what you are going through, there is always a scripture that relates to your situation. You can find comfort and peace in the Word of God. When we start reading the Word, God begins to purify us and make us more like Him. We begin to lose our sinful desires and begin to desire the things of God. Saturate yourself in the Word of God. It will direct your paths.

PRAYER

Heavenly Father, please help us to spend time in Your Word. Sometimes, we get so busy that we neglect reading our Bibles. However, Your Word is not only food for our spirit, but also a light that helps us stay on the right path. Help us to always find time to read Your Word, so that it will light our way. In Jesus' name. Amen.

Day 12

Spend Time in the Secret Place

He that dwelleth in the secret place of the most High shall abide under the shadow of the Almighty. (Psalm 91:1 – KJV).

As children of God, we need to dwell in the secret place. We need to spend time in the presence of the Lord. If we do, no evil will be able to prevail against us. The weapons will form, but they will not prosper (see Isaiah 54:17).

When we spend time in the presence of God, we are divinely protected. There is a constant battle in the spiritual realm.

The enemy comes to kill, to steal, and to destroy. He is relentless and will stop at nothing to destroy us. But when we abide in the presence of the Lord, the enemy doesn't stand a chance. God will dispatch His angels to protect you from the dangers that you are not even aware of (see Psalm 91:11).

Whenever the Israelites were obedient to God and dwelt in His presence, He gave them victory over their enemies. However, whenever they were disobedient, it led to their downfall. Spend time with the Lord. Develop a relationship with Him and dwell in His presence. He will protect you from all the traps of the enemy. The forces of hell will not be able to prevail against you. Spend time with the Lord. Get in the secret place.

PRAYER

Heavenly Father, thank You for Your divine protection. Thank You for protecting us in times when we didn't even realize we were in danger. Help us to keep seeking after You and to spend time with You. It is in the secret place that we receive Your blessings, including Your protection. May we continue to dwell in Your presence. In Jesus' name. Amen.

Day 13

Give Your Cares to God

Cast your cares on the Lord and He will sustain you; He will never let the righteous fall. (Psalm 55:22 – NIV).

We sometimes burn ourselves out trying to do everything on our own. But God wants us to cast our cares on Him. When we try to do everything on our own, it leaves us drained, exhausted, and disillusioned. Allow God to take the driver's seat. He knows the perfect destination. Allow Him to take full control. Leave everything in His hands and follow His leading. As the saying goes, *"If you leave everything in God's hands, you will see God's hand in everything."*

Trust in the Lord with all thine heart; and lean not unto thine own understanding. In all thy ways acknowledge him, and he shall direct thy paths. (Proverbs 3:5-6 – KJV).

Listen to that still, small voice that is speaking to you. God knows everything you need. He knows your hopes, dreams, and desires. Follow His leading and watch Him work things out in your favor. Trust God and leave everything in His hands. He will bless you in unexpected ways.

PRAYER

Heavenly Father, please help us to stop burning ourselves out trying to do everything on our own. Please help us to cast our cares on You so that You can sustain us. Please give us the rest we need. Please help us to trust You wholeheartedly, so that we can lower our guard and find rest in You. In Jesus' name. Amen.

Day 14

Rest in the Lord

Come to me all who labor and are heavy laden and I will give you rest. (Matthew 11:28 – ESV).

Sometimes we become burdened by the cares of life. We feel tired, stressed, and frustrated. Some people even feel like giving up.

Life is not easy, and we all have our struggles. Sometimes we fight until we have no fight left in us. God wants us to give our burdens to Him. He doesn't want us to bear them alone. God loves us and wants us to be prosperous and happy. He will help you bear your burdens. Just place them at His feet and leave them there. Not only will He help you to bear your burdens, but He will also give you peace that surpasses all understanding (see Philippians 4:7).

The problems won't disappear, but God will give you the strength to face them. You will be amazed at the level of peace and joy you feel when everything around you seems to be falling apart. Pray and leave everything in God's hands. He will lighten your load and give you rest. Put your trust in God and lay your burdens at His feet. He will help you weather the storms.

PRAYER

Heavenly Father, the pressures of life can leave us tired, drained, and frustrated. Please help us to place our burdens at Your feet and find rest in You. Please give us comfort and peace in whatever situations we are facing. In Jesus' name. Amen.

Day 15

Though We Fall, Yet We Rise Again

For though the righteous fall seven times, they rise again. (Proverbs 24:16 – NIV).

As children of God, you will receive the blessings and favor of the Lord. However, that doesn't mean that things will always go well. The devil prowls like a roaring lion looking for someone to devour (see 1 Peter 5:8). He is relentless and will stop at nothing to make you lose your way.

As Christians, we will fall short. No one is perfect, so we will mess up. That is why we should live a life of repentance. Whenever we fall, we must get up and continue our journey. We will encounter hard times. The devil throws obstacles in our way to discourage us and tempt us to give up. That's the time we need to be rooted and grounded in the Lord.

Even if you encounter setbacks or failure, know that the Lord is fighting for you. You will come out victorious. No matter what trials and tribulations may come your way, you will overcome. God will never give up on you, so don't give up on yourself. Continue fighting the good fight.

PRAYER

Heavenly Father, we are far from perfect and we fall more times than we care to remember. But we know that You will never give up on us, so we shouldn't give up on ourselves. Please help us to get back up whenever we fall, and to live a life of repentance. In Jesus' name. Amen.

Day 16

God's Love is Unconditional

For I am convinced that neither death nor life, neither angels nor demons, neither the present nor the future, nor any powers, neither height nor depth, nor anything else in all creation, will be able to separate us from the love of God that is in Christ Jesus our Lord. (Romans 8:38-39 – NIV).

God loves us so much. There is no love on earth that can compare to God's love for us. He loved us so much that He sent His only Son to die for us.

There may be times when we feel like we don't deserve God's love. We may mess up and fall short and think that God no longer loves us. But He is a God of love. He hates sin but loves the sinner. He may not always be pleased with the way we live or the things we do, but that will not make Him love us any less.

The enemy may try to confuse us, making us think that our past actions have caused God to no longer love us. That couldn't be further from the truth. There is nothing we can do that will stop Him from loving us. That doesn't mean He condones sin. We will still face the consequences of our sin unless we surrender our lives to God, walk in obedience to Him, and live a life of repentance. Just like our earthly parents will not stop loving us because of our mistakes, it is the same way with our heavenly Father. He loves us beyond measure.

PRAYER

Heavenly Father, thank You for Your constant love. Please help us to remember that Your love for us is unconditional, and we didn't have to earn it. In Jesus' name. Amen.

Day 17

There is Power in Worship

Worship the Lord your God and His blessing will be on your food and water. I will take away sickness from among you. (Exodus 23:25 – NIV).

There is power in worship. Some people may view worship as just singing a few gospel songs. But there is more to worship than that. True worship is a form of intimacy with God. During worship, we invite the presence of God into our lives.

We were created to worship God, so praise and worship is a form of communing with Him. We get to a deeper level with Him. Worship also invites angels. True praise and worship cause power to come down from heaven. Worship is very powerful. It has the power to tear down strongholds, release you from bondage, and bring healing and deliverance. Worship is a powerful weapon that many people take for granted.

In 2 Chronicles 20:21, King Jehoshaphat appointed singers to go ahead of the army, singing and praising God. The enemies were defeated, and the army of Judah didn't even have to draw their swords.

Worship is a powerful weapon. Use it in your day-to-day life and watch the hand of God work in your favor. The devil hates when we worship the Lord, which is even more reason to do it continually. The next time you are tempted to start worrying, start worshipping instead. Worship the Lord, and the blessings will flow.

PRAYER

Heavenly Father, may we always remember to worship You. Worship is a powerful weapon that weakens the enemy. Help us to always make time to worship You, especially when we don't feel like it. In Jesus' name. Amen.

Day 18

The Power of Belief

Therefore I say unto you, What things soever ye desire, when ye pray, believe that ye receive them, and ye shall have them. (Mark 11:24 – KJV).

When we ask God for something, we should believe that we have received it the moment we asked for it. That is a sign of faith. Many times we pray and ask God for something, and then we begin to wonder if it will happen. Sometimes we become impatient and begin to wonder when we will get it. We may even give up and say that God hasn't answered our prayer. However, the verse above instructs us to believe that we have received it. It means that we should see ourselves already having it. We should act as if we already have it. Start giving God thanks in advance. Even if it takes a while, continue to believe that you have received it.

After God promised Abraham a son, it took twenty-five years for the promise to be fulfilled. But Abraham didn't doubt God, and the promise came to fruition. We need to have faith that God will come through for us. It is normal to have doubts at times, but don't dwell on those doubts. Put your faith into action. Trust God and take Him at His Word.

PRAYER

Heavenly Father, please increase our faith. At times, we become doubtful or even frustrated when we are not seeing what we have prayed for. Help us to have unshakeable faith, so that even when we don't see our desires, we still believe that we have them. In Jesus' name. Amen.

Day 19

We Have Power and Authority in Jesus

Behold, I give unto you the power to tread on serpents and scorpions, and over all the power of the enemy: and nothing shall by any means hurt you. (Luke 10:19 – KJV).

God has given us power over the enemy. We do not need to fear him when we have authority over him. The devil and his legion of demons want us to fear them, but God is all-powerful, and He has equipped us with power over the enemy. However, we become powerless when we live a life of sin. That is why the enemy tries every way to lure us into sin. He knows that when we indulge in sin, we become spiritually weak, and then he can triumph over us. However, when we are spiritually strong, not even opposition from the gates of hell will be able to shake us.

God is our power source, and when we are plugged into Him, no force of evil will be able to triumph over us. We have no reason to fear the enemy when God has given us power over him. Jesus has already defeated him at the cross, so he has no power over God's children. Stay plugged in to God, and you will defeat the enemy.

PRAYER

Heavenly Father, please help us to remember that You have given us power and authority over the enemy. Therefore, we have no reason to fear him and his minions. You are in control, and as long as we live a life of obedience and stay connected to You, the enemy will not be able to triumph over us. In Jesus' name. Amen.

Day 20

All Things Are Working For Our Good

And we know that all things work together for good to them that love God, to them who are the called according to his purpose. (Romans 8:28 – KJV).

Sometimes, we face numerous challenges and struggles. We sometimes feel like we are at the end of our rope. But all things, both good and bad, work together for our good. God is very strategic. He allows things to happen for a reason. You may be facing a dark situation and think that God has forgotten you. Continue being faithful to Him and watch Him work things out in your favor.

Joseph endured years of suffering, even though he did nothing wrong. Through all his suffering, he remained faithful to God. As a result of his faithfulness, God moved him from the prison to the palace. He became second in command to King Pharaoh. No matter how dark the way may seem, God has a plan. Just trust Him and follow His leading. He will amaze you with His goodness. Put God first in every situation, and He will work everything out for your good.

PRAYER

Heavenly Father, sometimes it feels as if everything is going wrong. Please help us to remember that all things are working together for our good. When it feels like things are falling apart, You are behind the scenes working things out in our favor. May we always put our trust in You and allow You to do what only You can do. In Jesus' name. Amen.

Day 21

Do Not Be Distracted

"Martha, Martha," the Lord answered. "You are worried and upset about many things, but few things are needed – or indeed, only one. Mary has chosen what is better, and it will not be taken away from her." (Luke 10:41-42 – NIV).

When Jesus visited Martha's house, she was distracted by all the preparations. However, Mary sat at Jesus' feet, listening to him. Martha was upset that Mary wasn't helping her. But Jesus told her that Mary had chosen the better part.

Sometimes, we become so busy in our day-to-day lives that we neglect our relationship with God. We may even be so busy doing the work of God that it prevents us from having communion with Him. Our relationship with God should be our number one priority.

We all have important things to do, but spending time with God should always take priority. If we make time for God, He will help us accomplish all our other tasks. If we show up for Him, He will show up for us. Do not be like Martha, getting distracted by your various tasks. Strive to be like Mary and sit at Jesus' feet, and He will work things out in your favor.

PRAYER

Heavenly Father, in this fast-paced world, our hectic schedule sometimes gets in the way of us spending adequate time with You. Please help us to prioritize our relationship with You. Instead of trying to squeeze You into our day, may we start planning our days around You. In Jesus' name. Amen.

Day 22

All Things Are Possible

...with God all things are possible.
(Matthew 19:26 – KJV).

There is nothing too hard for God to do. We should never limit Him. If He could close the mouths of the lions for Daniel, part the Red Sea for Moses, let the sun stand still for Joshua, open the prison doors for Peter, bless Sarah with a baby in her old age, and raise Lazarus from the dead, is there anything that He cannot do? He's the same God yesterday, today, and forevermore. If He could do it for them, He can do it for us.

We need to exercise our faith and trust Him wholeheartedly. You may be facing a situation that seems impossible. You may be climbing a mountain that seems insurmountable. You may be facing your own Red Sea situation. Just trust God. Surrender to His will and have complete faith in Him. He will work things out in ways that will blow your mind. If He did it before, He can do it again. Put God first, trust Him, and do your part, and He will work wonders in your life. He'll take you places you've never dreamed of.

PRAYER

Heavenly Father, sometimes we have doubts and place limits on You. Help us to remember that nothing is impossible for You. You worked great and mighty miracles in the past, and You can do it again. Help us to surrender to Your will and trust You wholeheartedly. In Jesus' name. Amen.

Day 23

We Need Each Other

As iron sharpens iron, so one person sharpens another. (Proverbs 27:17 – NIV).

There is an old adage that says, *"No man is an island."* That is quite true. We all need companionship. Furthermore, we need people who have our best interests at heart. Such persons will help to keep us accountable, tell us when we are wrong, and cheer us on when we do well.

As children of God, we need to be around like-minded persons. We need to be around people who are also diligently seeking the Lord. That way, we can help hold each other accountable and strengthen one another. Even introverted persons or self-professed "loners" need to have someone in their corner. Sometimes you may feel burdened or tired, and feel like giving up. A word of encouragement may be all you need to feel revived.

We are humans, and there are times we will have a moment of weakness. That is why we need a brother and/or sister to set us straight. We may feel like they are attacking us, but they are only trying to keep us in line. Let us start being our brothers' keeper. Let us help to sharpen each other.

PRAYER

Heavenly Father, help us to look out for each other. It is our duty to help bear each other's burdens. We need a support system, so please bless us with genuine people who have our best interests at heart. Help us to sharpen each other. In Jesus' name. Amen.

Day 24

God is Our Healer

But if the Spirit of him that raised up Jesus from the dead dwell in you, he that raised up Christ from the dead shall also quicken your mortal bodies by his Spirit that dwelleth in you. (Romans 8:11 – KJV).

Sickness is not of God. It is God's desire for us to prosper and be in good health (see 3 John 1:2). Jesus Christ took all our sins and infirmities to the cross. God wants us to be healthy and prosperous. However, the reality is that we are sometimes afflicted with sickness. Sometimes we resign ourselves to accepting our health situation, believing that it will not change. That is the time we need to exercise our faith. We may pray and not see any results, so we think that God has not answered our prayers. We need to stand on the promises of God. He promised us good health, so we need to keep meditating on healing scriptures. After praying, tell yourself that you are healed. Thank God every day for your healing. If you continually tell yourself that you are sick, you will likely remain so. Trust God and take Him at His Word. He is the Great Physician. There is nothing too hard for Him to do.

PRAYER

Heavenly Father, You are the Great Physician. You are Jehovah Rapha, our healer. Please increase our faith in You. You are still in the healing business, and You are ready to heal us from our infirmities. Sometimes it's our lack of faith that keeps us sick. Help us to receive Your healing that You freely give. In Jesus' name. Amen.

Day 25

Keep Your Focus on God

No temptation has overtaken you except what is common to mankind. And God is faithful; He will not let you be tempted beyond what you can bear. But when you are tempted, He will also provide a way out so that you can endure it. (1 Corinthians 10:13 – NIV).

Many people are of the view that when you give your life to God, it will be smooth sailing. That couldn't be further from the truth. When we get saved, that is when the devil puts us on his hit list. He wants us to stay in sin, and will do anything to keep us there.

When we decide to live for God, the devil will use all the weapons in his arsenal to prevent us from growing spiritually. We need to fight back with prayer, the Word of God, worship, and fasting. It is also essential that we put on the whole armor of God (see Ephesians 6:10-18). Whatever area we struggle with, that is where the enemy will hit the hardest.

At times, the temptations may seem too hard to bear. That is why we need to stay in the presence of God and saturate ourselves in His Word. There will always be trials and temptations, but stay focused on God, and He will strengthen you. Without a test, there would be no testimony. Rely on the Lord for strength. He will carry you through.

PRAYER

Heavenly Father, please give us the strength to persevere through our struggles. We all have our cross to bear. Please help us stay rooted and grounded in You, so that we may withstand the fiery darts of the enemy. In Jesus' name. Amen.

Day 26

God is Limitless

I can do all things through Christ which strengtheneth me. (Philippians 4:13 – KJV).

We sometimes place limits on ourselves, thinking that certain things are out of our reach. You may feel like you are going around in circles or climbing a mountain that seems insurmountable. Our circumstances or past experiences can make us feel like we are incapable of doing or accomplishing the things we desire. But is anything too hard for God to do?

Don't place limits on God. He is able to do the impossible. We sometimes try to do everything in our own strength, and then become frustrated when things don't work out the way we want them to. Put God first and allow Him to take control. He will work things out in ways you cannot imagine. He is all-knowing, and He knows what is best for us, so trust Him with your plans, hopes, dreams, and desires. He will make a way where there seems to be no way. He will resurrect dead situations. He will move you from the back of the line to the front. There is nothing He cannot do.

Friend, stop burning yourselves out trying to do everything on your own. Allow God to take control and watch things work out in your favor. You will realize that you can accomplish great things once you give God the lead. You will become unstoppable.

PRAYER

Heavenly Father, please help us to remember that we can accomplish great things with You by our side. Please continue to work in and through us. In Jesus' name. Amen.

Day 27

Lead by Example

Let your light shine before others, so that they may see your good works and give glory to your Father who is in heaven. (Matthew 5:16 – ESV).

As children of God, we are called to let our light shine, so that we may lead others to the Lord. It is very important for us to spread the gospel. But it is equally important to live a life that is pleasing to God. We can sometimes win souls for Christ not by what we say but by how we live. If we tell people about living for God and we are not living righteously, it will turn them off, and you may end up pushing them further away from God. We need to practice what we preach. We should not preach about one thing and then live our lives in a way that contradicts our words. We must be cautious not to mislead others.

God is not mocked, and we will all give an account for every idle word we speak (see Matthew 12:36). When we are living righteously and start bearing fruit, people will see the glory of God on us. When others see you go through the fire and come out as pure gold, it may be the push they need to give their lives to God. The life you live can show others the goodness and glory of God. Action speaks louder than words. Let your actions and lifestyle show others who God is.

PRAYER

Heavenly Father, please help us to live our lives in a way that will lead others to You. May we let our light shine and be a beacon of hope for others in this dark world. In Jesus' name. Amen.

Day 28

Forgiveness is Essential

For if ye forgive men their trespasses, your heavenly Father will also forgive you: But if ye forgive not men their trespasses, neither will your Father forgive your trespasses. (Matthew 6:14-15 – KJV).

It is important to forgive others. It is sometimes easier said than done, but if you want to be right with God, it is necessary. When Peter asked Jesus if he should forgive his brother who sins against him seven times, Jesus told him no, not seven times, but seventy times seven (see Matthew 18:21-22). That means we should forgive others repeatedly. It is not always easy. We sometimes experience such hurt and betrayal that it cuts deep, and we vow never to forgive the person who hurt us. However, holding on to hurt and resentment is toxic. Let it go if you want to have peace. Furthermore, if we do not forgive others, our heavenly Father will not forgive us. After all, we often commit sins that break God's heart, yet He is always willing to forgive us. Is it unreasonable for us to do the same?

Friend, learn to forgive others. It will give you peace, and God will be pleased.

PRAYER

Heavenly Father, please help us to have a forgiving heart. Help us to forgive others just as You have forgiven us. Harboring unforgiveness will harm us not only spiritually but also physically. Please help us to release all unforgiveness. In Jesus' name. Amen.

Day 29

God Will Put Your Enemies to Shame

You prepare a table before me in the presence of my enemies, You anoint my head with oil; my cup overflows. (Psalm 23:5 – NIV).

In this life, you will have enemies. It's inevitable. You don't have to be a bad person to have enemies. People will dislike you just for being the way you are. They may try to tear you down and poison other people's minds against you. Don't retaliate or try to fight fire with fire. Just pray and leave everything to God.

Jesus said we should love our enemies and pray for those who despitefully use and persecute us. Always be the bigger person. God will reward you for it. He will bless you in front of your enemies. Your enemies may plot your demise and try every way to tear you down. They may criticize and slander you and even spread false rumors about you. But when you are favored by God, all the plots and schemes of your enemies will fail. The more they fight against you, the more God will elevate you. Little do they know that when they fight against a child of God, they are literally fighting against God. He will put them to shame. Leave your battles to God. He will shower His blessings on you in the presence of your enemies.

PRAYER

Heavenly Father, please help us to be unperturbed by the plots of our enemies. Please help us to leave everything in Your hands. In due season, You will elevate us for our enemies to see. In Jesus' name. Amen.

Day 30

God Will Blow Your Mind

Now unto him that is able to do exceeding abundantly above all that we ask or think, according to the power that worketh in us. (Ephesians 3:20 – KJV).

In our walk with God, we often limit ourselves by what we can see, understand, or imagine. But Ephesians 3:20 reminds us that God's power far surpasses our human understanding. He is able to do *"exceedingly abundantly above all that we ask or think."*

We sometimes place limits on God. We think a goal or a dream is too big, but God specializes in the supernatural and the extraordinary. He can work things out in ways far greater than you can imagine. Just trust Him and live a life of obedience. His capacity to bless, provide, and work in our lives is limitless. He desires to exceed our expectations, surpass our hopes, and shower us with abundance beyond measure. His power working in us enables us to achieve the impossible, overcome the unimaginable, and receive the uncontainable.

Let us expand our faith, broaden our horizons, and trust in God's exceeding abundance. May we glorify Him in our lives, and may His power work in us to impact generations. We have plans for ourselves, but God has far bigger plans for us. Just abide in Him and watch the blessings flow. He will blow your mind.

PRAYER

Heavenly Father, thank You for Your limitless power and abundance. Help us to trust in Your exceeding greatness and surrender our lives to Your mighty work. May your glory shine through us and may we be a testament to Your abundant grace. In Jesus' name. Amen.

Final Thoughts

As we conclude this 30-Day journey together, remember that God's love and presence are always with you. May the truths and insights you've gained during this time continue to guide and inspire you in the days ahead.

Hold on to the hope and promises of God's Word, and don't hesitate to return to these devotions whenever you need encouragement or guidance.

Most importantly, remember that your faith journey is unique, and God has a special plan and purpose for your life. Continue to seek Him, trust Him, and follow Him, and you will find peace, joy, and fulfillment in His presence.

May God bless you richly as you continue on your spiritual journey.

Author Bio

Allan Lynfester is a passionate writer, poet, and storyteller who has dedicated his life to inspiring and ministering to others through the written word. With twenty years of writing experience, Allan has crafted works across multiple genres, including poetry, fiction, non-fiction, and plays. He strongly believes that God has blessed him with this gift to uplift, encourage, and bring people closer to Him.

As an accomplished writer, Allan has received 21 awards in the JCDC Creative Writing Competition, a testament to his dedication and skill. Additionally, two of his poems have been published in The Sunday Gleaner, showcasing his ability to touch hearts through poetry. His work reflects his deep faith and desire to share God's love with the world.

Abiding in Him: Devotions for a Deeper Connection is his first published book, a devotional designed to help readers strengthen their relationship with God. Through scripture-based reflections, heartfelt encouragement, and thought-provoking insights, Allan hopes to inspire others to embrace the blessings of faith and obedience.

Beyond writing, Allan is a trained social worker who is deeply committed to helping others find hope, purpose, and encouragement in their daily lives. He sees his writing as an extension of his ministry, using words to bring light, healing, and spiritual transformation.

Stay connected with Allan Lynfester:
Email: allanlynfester@gmail.com

Follow on Social Media: @AllanLynfester on TikTok, Instagram, and Facebook.

Allan invites you to join him on this journey of faith, inspiration, and storytelling.

Stay tuned for more books, devotionals, and creative works that aim to uplift and encourage!

www.ingramcontent.com/pod-product-compliance
Lightning Source LLC
LaVergne TN
LVHW051158080426
835508LV00021B/2688